BREAKING POINT

A Chistian Guide to Addiction Intervention

by Robert and Stephanie Tucker

Breaking Point: A Christian Guide to Intervention
Written by Robert and Stephanie Tucker

Published by
Spirit of Life Recovery Resources
18652 Florida Street, Suite 200
Huntington Beach, CA 92648

All monies from this book purchase will help accomplish our mission. Spirit of Life Recovery supports people struggling with emotional and spiritual challenges, including addiction and codependence. Spirit of Life Recovery is a 501 (c)(3) non-profit Christian Ministry—Fed tax #27-3278002. To learn more, visit www.spiritofliferecovery.com.

The stories and examples may or may not be based on actual clinical situations; however, where applicable, names were changed to protect privacy. This book is not necessarily intended to diagnose or treat your individual issues. If you are in a serious or life-threatening situation, please get professional help immediately. This book is by no means intended to replace the need for professional and/or medical treatment. This book is an opinion. You are free to accept or reject our opinion.

For grammar, editorial, or any other issues pertaining to the quality of the production of this workbook, please contact the publisher, Spirit of Life Recovery, directly.

Printed in the United States of America.

Editing by www.ChristianEditingServices.com.

TABLE OF CONTENTS

-1-
The Breaking Point

Family members of an addict feel overwhelmed, exhausted, and chained to the chronic fear of the next looming crisis. They feel betrayed, used, and wounded financially, relationally, emotionally, and even spiritually by the addiction that has taken control of their loved one's life. They have made efforts to help, rescue, and change their loved one. But despite their best intentions, the cycle of addiction repeats over and over again.

Addictive behavior takes many forms and has different meanings depending on its unique circumstances. But in a basic way, an addiction occurs whenever a person exhibits a compulsion that causes him or her to engage in risky and unhealthy behavior to obtain the next high. Addicts cannot stop using their drug or behavior of choice, even though they often insist they have no problem. This inability to stop is called bondage. Usually, the addictions that inflict the most damage involve chemical abuse or unhealthy sexual behaviors, but they can extend to many other behaviors.

Addictive behavior is maddening and confounding. It's like watching someone with a fatal love affair give up everything and everyone just to satisfy the object of an obsession. The behavior will consume that person's every thought, desire, and driving motivation. And in its fiery trail it leaves the carnage of lies, manipulation, deceitfulness, and devastation. Anyone who has experienced addiction has a personal account of exactly what that means. And as millions of others who have dealt with the ravages of this cycle will tell you, there will come a breaking point.

While it's of vital importance you learn about addiction and the nature of the substance or activity involved, it's just as important you understand some critical intervention principles. These will not just help your loved one who has a problem but also will offer you a means to focus on a solution to maintain your sense of well-being.

THE STORM OF ADDICTION

If you've been walking beside an active addict, chances are you've sometimes felt you were losing your mind. The insanity of addiction is a full-force tornado sweeping through your life and wreaking havoc in its path. In truth, whether you choose it or not, you've been hit by the addict's lifestyle. And in efforts to help, fix, and protect that person, you find yourself in the midst of relentless winds trying to glue broken pieces together. Truth be told, it doesn't work.

Doing nothing surely can't be a better option, can it? The problem is, you feel overpowered—you feel that addiction is enormous and has stolen the precious person you love and the dreams you carry in your heart. You are fighting for that person, and you are fighting for his or her future.

Or perhaps you feel beyond hope. You are just trying to survive the wreckage of the past years the best you know how. Life is dulled by the addiction's endless demands and its oppressive grip. But is living in a demolished home the life God designed? Of course not. The questions, then, are twofold: How can you handle the addiction, and what are your options?

If you are in a supportive role with the addict in your life, please know that your desire to help is noble and good. But maintaining sanity in the midst of the storm requires a different approach. And, to be honest, you can rebuild with or without that person involved. That's because there are methods for taking back control from the addict. You can essentially leave the tornado and do your part from the sidelines.

Your decision to do so will have various challenges. You will need to ask yourself, if you could leave the storm and find retreat, would you? Or do you fear leaving ________________ behind? Do you feel so victimized by ________________ that leaving seems impossible? These are very tough questions you probably can't answer right now, but it's vital you address them at some point.

When we discuss leaving the storm of someone's addiction, we don't necessarily mean leaving the relationship; we mean no longer participating in its insanity. We shouldn't fall into the common trap of thinking that Christian love means we should tolerate and live with someone's sinful and unhealthy lifestyle. Please understand, it is good to want to steer someone out of harm's way, but you must recognize when that person's wrongful behavior is taking you down too. That doesn't mean we can't fight for someone. The Bible puts it this way:

> "Dear brothers and sisters, if another believer is overcome by some sin, you who are godly should gently and humbly help that person back onto the right path. And be careful not to fall into the same temptation yourself" (Galatians 6:1).

Being able to assist in an addict's restoration without allowing that person's lifestyle to cause us to stumble takes precision and wisdom. We may not have the temptation of the addiction, but we can get dragged down with it in other ways—control, anger, resentment, to name a few.

The purpose of this resource is to help you identify the means to intervene without becoming bogged down and injured by someone else's negative lifestyle. Furthermore, it will offer you a method to secure your own well-being, even if doing so feels uncomfortable.

NOT ME

You might not want to make yourself part of the discussion right now. After all, ____________ has the problem. But the truth is, it has affected you. To help you see this influence in more detail, we encourage you to read this scenario, playing it out in your mind, and see if you can relate.

Close your eyes and imagine being inside a plane that needs to make an emergency crash landing. The cabin starts to lose oxygen. You are gripped with terror as you realize breathing is becoming difficult, and you fumble to grab your oxygen mask. In the chaos, you notice a young girl and a baby who need your assistance. You feel heartbroken for them and are moved with compassion. You move over to aid them until you feel a quick drop, and you realize you are close to passing out. You have to make a dramatic choice: Do you secure their oxygen masks or your own? How can you be selfish in the midst of such a crisis? You only have a split second to decide, and then the words suddenly pop into your head: "Before assisting with someone else's mask, be sure to secure your own." You quickly place the mask onto your face and begin to inhale deep breaths. With the oxygen fueling your body, you now feel empowered to help those who can't help themselves.

Now think of your crisis with addiction. It's like that plane heading for a wreck and running out of oxygen. You and the addict are both suffocating, but that person seems ignorant of his or her options. You can consume yourself with efforts to aid and rescue your loved one, at the expense of your own needs. Or you can connect to a life source and gain the tools and wisdom to understand how you can help both yourself and ____________.

This process is a means of empowerment—it's your oxygen mask, so to speak. It is meant to uplift and encourage you in the crisis of addiction so that you can be strengthened to make choices.

Yes, we are going to address your loved one's addiction in this material. But no, fixing them and giving everything you have isn't the solution. You will learn more about what truly helping an addict involves, but more than likely it will mean finding additional support resources. If you have those resources accessible right now, use them! This might mean seeking a meeting with other parents or spouses of addicts that is specific to your situation (alcohol, drugs, sex, etc.). It might be securing a counselor or a mentor. You might just need to reach out to a trusted friend. Whatever that help looks like for you, allow that lifeline to assist you.

Action Step:

What can I do right now to be supported?

____

____

____

Have I been giving out of lack? Have I been suffocating?

____

____

____

____

____

____

____

____

____

-2-
Confronting Addiction's Realities

Addiction is so severe because it blinds the person under its influence. Other people can see clearly the problem, but the addict refuses to acknowledge it. Sometimes family members are blinded too, either because they don't know how to face the truth or because they have just learned to adjust to life with the addiction's presence, normalizing its effect. Others are in situations where they don't know how to live without the addict's support emotionally or financially. Thus, they feel forced to comply with addiction's harsh demands.

When cycles are created, it takes an intervention to disrupt them. Intervention challenges wrongful behaviors when circumstances are out of control. It causes a sense of urgency that something must change. For addicts, an intervention is meant to be a wake-up call to make them face reality.

If you are contemplating this process but are scared of the risks and don't have the knowledge, we'll begin to walk you through various options. But it won't replace the need for professional help at some point in certain situations.

THE PURPOSE OF INTERVENTION

If you've ever watched TV shows about interventions, you'll immediately think of dramatic scenes of addiction, chaos, and efforts to force people into treatment programs. An intervention can indeed involve an established event, as we will discuss later. However, we are going to learn in this material that real intervention is instigated in the heart and initiated by God's power, not by human strength. Its purpose is to allow God to intervene in someone's life. This kind of intervention goes beyond anything we can perform. However, we can partner with God and simply do our part as he allows.

Intervention isn't an effort to control someone to act a certain way. It's a confrontation of truth, done in love, that lays out objectives and boundaries in the relationship. It deals with reality even though reality might be uncomfortable. We will discuss intervention in a deeper, more systematic fashion simply because a change of behavior will not fix everything immediately.

Most families believe that once the addict stops using the drug or behavior of choice, everything will be fixed. But in truth, that drug or behavior was merely a symptom of far deeper issues. In fact, without recovery, that person may act similarly or even worse without the addiction. Thus, while the intervention begins due to compulsive behavior, it needs to follow a pathway where the heart can be changed and influenced by God Almighty. Only he has access to the heart and the resources that permanently change human beings.

EDUCATING YOURSELF WITH FACTS

To get started, you should learn more about the nature of the addiction your loved one is facing. Education can be terribly unnerving, especially if you've avoided it out of fear, but it's absolutely necessary. If you are dealing with a person abusing drugs or alcohol, it's critical you learn the precise nature of what that drug does. If you are dealing with a behavioral addiction such as anger or sex, you'll need to understand there is much more happening than simply the outward behaviors.

You may have varying beliefs regarding what addiction is, and if you don't know the facts, you may be setting up unrealistic expectations. For example, many Christians see addiction as a moral choice alone. They say the addict is sinning and needs to repent, and they don't look beyond that. However, dealing with addiction as sin alone isn't enough because there are typically deeper-rooted issues that need a solution in order for true healing to occur. As Christians, we do believe the root of addiction is a sinful stronghold initiated by a demonic agenda that preys on personal areas of weakness, hurt, vulnerability, and pain. Therefore, it's vital to know the battle being waged.

First, you must understand that addiction is compulsive behavior that changes the brain, affects the entire body's ability to stabilize pain and mood, and disrupts the capacity to be in healthy relationships with self and others. It is a spiritual and soul sickness of the heart that places the mind and body in bondage. Addiction isn't just one thing; it's all-encompassing. By researching and understanding the scope of the particular addiction your loved one is dealing with, you will gain valuable information that will expand your understanding.

__________________ isn't his or her addiction; that person has an addiction, and it's replacing who he or she is. Thus, you need to arm yourself with the facts. Are you willing to crack open the door and pursue information specific to that addiction? Then start doing that right now!

Action Step:
What addiction am I facing right now?

____
____
____

Do I understand what that means in a factual way? How can I learn more right now?

____
____
____
____
____

-3-
The Power of Surrender

When you've learned about addiction and its compulsive tendencies, you can start to understand you've been up against the impossible. Even now, you might think, If I can say or do the right thing, I can make ________________ quit. Then you try that, and you get even worse results. It can be very frustrating.

That's why it's vital to understand that the addiction is stronger than the addict. At first, drugs and alcohol or addictive behaviors are fun or provide relief to addicts. But over time, the fun is a full-time job. It becomes a never-ending hunt to access the next high. Simply put, that addiction controls them. That's why you are astonished by their behavior and attitudes. They are in bondage to drugs or alcohol (or other behaviors), and that bondage makes them serve the need at any and all costs.

Therefore, the first and most important step in any recovery process is the acknowledgment of powerlessness toward the addiction itself. Step one in twelve-step programs says the following:

> "We admitted we were powerless over our addiction—that our lives had become unmanageable."

In full swing, addicts have no idea how powerful their disease is until they come to the place of recognizing their weakness. As we'll learn shortly, this truth helps us tremendously in learning our role. But the important thing to ask yourself is, how have you been dragged through addiction? What have you done to try to overcome addiction in someone's life? Go back to step one, and read it this way: "I admit I am powerless over ______________ and my life has become unmanageable." One of your intervention tools is your ability to accept that statement as personal truth. In fact, you may want to write that somewhere you can see it and remind yourself of it throughout the day. It may not feel good, but please don't let that discourage you. If you can recognize that you can't control _______________, you'll be positioned for what we know is biblical surrender. It may feel like defeat but not when you are surrendering to God.

Surrender is the opposite of effort. It means you openly acknowledge your inability to conquer your circumstances. You start by saying, "I can't." Surrender is a mindset—we place our trust and hope in God rather than ourselves. We wait expectantly for his leadership to guide us. We are not out on the front line dictating what the next step should look like. Instead, we sit until we hear the command.

When we attempt to fix things ourselves, we don't recognize our limitations and vulnerabilities. We are like a child taking off down the highway on a tricycle. That child is up against the impossible—and is in a place of extreme danger.

God sees us in the same way. No matter how fast and hard we pedal, we can never reach our destination. Why? Because it's a power struggle, not an issue of effort. Our little tricycle has no engine and no power. It wasn't designed to be on the highway. In the same way, even at our very best, we are overpowered by the nature of addiction. We need God to rescue us in the vehicle of his grace. But God isn't judging us; he wants us to let him help us with deeper compassion and mercy. He knows our situation, and he also knows only he can handle it.

Being in God's hand doesn't require skill or super-religious status. It just requires surrender—the act of connecting, which in turn is simply an act of trust and faith. Like an appliance requiring power to operate, we learn that it's our primary job to plug into God, not to try to solve problems in our strength. This involves relationship building, which may be a need in your life you are not sure how to develop. That is part of your journey.

When it comes to the lifestyle of addiction, our efforts stem from a desire to help someone we value and love. To surrender leaves us in a vulnerable state. It makes us feel powerless, and it takes away any security that we can somehow alter this situation. We suddenly feel the weight of "what if." When we are taking action, we can feel that we are in some way changing the outcome. This is extremely challenging because surrender is our own personal intervention moment in which we have to face the truth that "I can't."

Submitting to surrender, however, isn't about giving up or leaving the relationship. It's an act of transferring the person we love from our care into

God's hands. Surrender is a state of dependence on God's resources rather than our own. But that's where you can gain clarity, hope, and strength. Surrender is where God's power starts to be activated on your behalf. It goes like this: "I can't. God, help me." The Bible says it this way:

> "My grace is sufficient for you, for my power is made perfect in weakness" (2 Corinthians 12:9 NIV).

You may want to post that Bible passage someplace visible to remind you that God is most interested in your weakness, not in your strength. What a backward way to think! But it truly unlocks the beginning of personal freedom and hope.

BE STILL

Surrender is easiest when we can get quieted internally. We often don't realize how loud the noise of crisis becomes when each day brings new drama. Getting quiet is where you will most easily find God. It may require you find a totally private place where you can create a sanctuary. In stillness and quietness, that connection can be formed. The reason is that trust and faith bring us into God's strength, whereas personal effort and busyness typically keep us away. The Bible says this: "Only in returning to me and resting in me will you be saved. In quietness and confidence is your strength" (Isaiah 30:15).

Action Step:
Music is one of the best ways to calm our spirit. Find a quiet place where you have access to download a song. You can pick any music you know that will quiet your heart. One of our favorites is Casting Crowns's "Just Be Held." We encourage you to listen to this song and meditate on the words.

As you listen, try to visualize somehow giving yourself to Jesus. Maybe you hold his hand or sit next to him. Maybe he picks you up and carries you. You don't need to read the Bible at this moment (although we encourage separate devotional time) because it's all about connecting. If this seems hard, don't worry. You can't get it wrong.

When we begin to connect to God, we may also feel emotions being uncovered. No matter the emotion, let it out. You may want to write the emotion out so you better understand and define it. The start to your own healing depends upon your ability to purge what's going on in your heart.

-4-
Loving a Person, Hating Addiction

An addict's behavior hurts us. It injures us and messes with our sense of identity and worth. Addicts hurl lies and accusations at anyone they can in order to allow someone else to bear the weight of their mistakes. But addicts aren't only hurting us; they are also self-destructing. They are killing themselves.

Why would anyone do this? Obviously, it's not normal behavior. The Bible tells us this truth: "The thief's purpose is to steal and kill and destroy. My purpose is to give them a rich and satisfying life" (John 10:10).

There is always a battle lurking behind the scenes. Anyone engaged in destructive behavior is being influenced by the enemy. While the addict will feel like your enemy, don't be deceived. That person isn't the enemy; instead, you share the same enemy. You also share the same Father. If your loved one doesn't know Jesus, God is still that person's Creator and wants to be his or her Redeemer. You share in that desire together.

When you look at God's agenda, you find that he is trying to give life and love; the enemy is the one trying to take it away. Thus, your job is to side with everything God would do to declare war on addiction.

To love someone who offers nothing in return can feel unjust. And that's because it is. We are recipients of the unjust love of Jesus Christ, who relentlessly sought us out when we had nothing to offer. Yes, that means at one point we were an intervention project, and Jesus got hold of us! God calls us to move with that same love. Thus, he doesn't guarantee justice when he asks us to love a person struggling with addiction.

Before you moan at this harsh and seemingly unkind truth, remember that loving a person isn't accepting, condoning, or allowing that one's bad behavior. Remember, God loves the person and wants to kill the addiction.

He would never allow the very thing that would take a person out! Not only that, but he would never condone someone's abuse of you! It's not okay to be misused, abused, lied to, hurt, and betrayed. No, you don't need to dish out more money and bail out your loved one another time from careless and irresponsible choices. No! No! No! That's not what love is!

The question then remains: How do we love a person while wanting to murder the thing that is bringing horrible destruction? Our first task in the role of love is simply to get out of God's way. It is deeply humbling to do this. When someone goes astray, God will use discipline to attempt to draw him or her back. But if we aren't careful, we can use our own version of love to remove the very disciplines God has placed as divine opportunities to bring forth change in the addict.

If you struggle to define love, you can be assured that in regard to an addict, your love will always revolve around wanting him or her free from addiction. What we may need to adjust is how we think that freedom can be attained. Only Jesus has the role of the Savior of the human heart. We should embrace anything that will allow our loved one to encounter him, and we should reject anything that drives and enables the wrongful behaviors to continue.

Separating addiction (behavior) from a person is very difficult—it's why we must surrender first. We honestly can't do that in our strength. It's also why we need the tools of intervention we will continue to explore. To sum it all up, we might say it this way: "Love is siding with God for a person's well-being." Soon we are going to start learning exactly how that is done.

A FRIEND CALLED PAIN

While addiction is the enemy we want to murder, pain is the friend we need to learn to embrace. Addicts run from pain, and so do we. Not only that, but we also try to shield those we love from pain. It is second nature to protect ourselves and those we love. In fact, we seem like experts in learning how to flee pain and look for ways to soothe it. However, pain is the critical key to unlocking a healthy partnership with God as we move toward intervention.

As already mentioned, God disciplines those he loves. He also uses pain as a tool to alert us that something is wrong and needs to be fixed, whether it be physical, emotional, or spiritual. Without pain, we would never have a way to perceive that we need help. This works for us when there is a physical ailment in our body: pain drives us to seek help. For example, if your arm is broken, you'll have intense pain, and you'll need to get it treated. If you have heart pain, you need to go to a hospital to diagnose the cause. If all our pain sensors broke at one time, it might seem to be a wonderful miracle—until we start suffering from injury, infection, and illness for which we sought no help because we have no pain to warn us to get help. The lack of pain didn't help; in fact, it may kill us.

Your ability to allow someone to feel pain may be one of your greatest life challenges ever. Please understand: those who medicate through addiction have a pain problem. Addiction is an escape—a quick shortcut to ease pain and bring immediate pleasure. If you are dealing with someone who is using a chemical substance, that person has tricked his or her body to eliminate pain in a destructive way. The body loses touch with its pain and can't appropriately warn that person that something is wrong. Nonchemical addictions also work to overly stimulate pleasure (as in cases of sex addiction) or to numb pain (as in cases of anger addiction). Simply put, they are all pain problems.

Addicts' inability to feel pain allows them to reward themselves with whatever benefit the drug or addiction brings, only to stuff the nature of the problem down deeper. For example, Todd likes to get high. It feels good and helps him avoid life, responsibility, and his deep-down sense of insecurity. That's the benefit. The drug isn't working when it creates more pain than it soothes. When the pain of addiction outweighs the benefits, often help is sought. For Todd, his high is harder and harder to attain, and he begins to steal and finds himself making horrible choices. Then he's arrested. He feels the pain of that circumstance, and suddenly the drug's benefits are lessened, and the pain it causes is heightened. He's now ready for change.

Addicts are ready to get help not because someone kept rescuing them from pain but because pain beat them down to a place of desperation. Could they kill themselves first? Of course, and that's where you need to assess the severity. You may be amazed at how much pain can be endured while the addict remains faithful to the addiction.

Typically, if you see an addict remain in stubbornness and denial, you know more pain is required. Thus, you should befriend pain as God's tool to take someone through the journey toward the solution. If you see the addict start to show signs of change and then fall into old patterns, begin to pray for pain.

The Bible instructs us with these truths about pain:

> For the kind of sorrow God wants us to experience leads us away from sin and results in salvation. There's no regret for that kind of sorrow.

> But worldly sorrow, which lacks repentance, results in spiritual death. (2 Corinthians 7:10)
>
> Now I am glad I sent it, not because it hurt you, but because the pain caused you to repent and change your ways. It was the kind of sorrow God wants his people to have, so you were not harmed by us in any way. (2 Corinthians 7:9)
>
> No discipline is enjoyable while it is happening—it's painful! But afterward, there will be a peaceful harvest of right living for those who are trained in this way. (Hebrews 12:11)

How exactly do you assist in helping pain have its way? We are going to learn that next.

-5-
When to Help, When not to Help

You may be seeing things that are difficult, so it's time to say this: be kind to yourself. Be understanding. You have done what you needed to do. It's okay. Today is a new day and a new chance. Some of this will be difficult to hear, but remember, it's your intervention too. And that's a good thing. Jesus loves you enough to have you in this place right here, right now. Know that

God is on your side. He is for you, not against you. He loves you and the person you are struggling with. He sees the entire picture.

As you move into intervention, this next step can feel brutal. But it has one primary objective: to let pain take effect. If you have befriended pain, what does that mean? Simply put, you agree with pain's agenda. You say, "Go ahead, pain; have your way."

Family members who block pain create barriers rather than pathways toward redemption. Of course, they don't do this intentionally. The only way for you to know if you are in any way participating in blocking pain is to examine how you interact in your relationship.

Facing the ways you may have encouraged addiction rather than helped disable it is a courageous step! No matter how you've interacted with addicts in the past, remember: their responses are not your fault. You are never responsible for the actions of others, but you can get swept up in the cycle of them. Let's take a look at how this can occur.

We simply intervene in the wrong thing: we remove the consequences of the addict's bad behavior when those consequences may be the very things that would set him or her free.

Poor choices yield negative results; that's one of the best growth tools available. Mistakes, failure, and bad choices create experiences that can shape us to make better choices in the future. Thus, when we intervene in the area of natural consequences, we prevent someone's growth and maturity.

For instance, Jeff kept spending money to support his habit. While his mother was aware of his addiction, she continued to be manipulated. When he couldn't pay his rent or afford to buy his favorite concert ticket, Jeff's mom paid it for him. Jeff had no motivation to quit. He had the best of both worlds.

We continue to take responsibility for the addict's problems rather than let him or her bear that weight.

Family members are sometimes more concerned about the addict's situation than the addict is. In the addiction cycle, addicts are often numbed and unaware of the complete chaos and insanity they create.

For example, when Julie received a drunk-driving ticket and was put in jail, her mother was frantic. She drove four hours to claim Julie's car, have it towed and repaired, and post bail money. As Julie came out of jail, she was disrespectful and rude, with no appreciation for her mom's efforts. She immediately went out drinking, all while her mother secured an expensive lawyer to bail her out of her bad choices. Julie didn't need to own her problems because her mother carried them for her.

We allow the addict's denial to become our reality, rather than see the truth of the situation.

Denial is a powerful force that demands everyone to respond to it. Denial forces members to view addiction through the addict's perspective rather than deal with the addiction. When addiction becomes the voice of truth, everyone involved will feel insane—literally.

Tom's addiction was ruling the home as he terrorized the family with all the things they were doing wrong. The focus and blame were continually placed on them throughout the day, giving Tom permission to continue his addiction. The family obliged and agreed with him, thus helping perpetuate that denial. They were too afraid and beaten down to oppose Tom. Outside help was needed for them as well as for Tom.

Denial may have aided them at the moment, but it, in turn, created weakness, despair, and an imprisoned environment. No one—not one single person on this earth—has the right to dictate truth to you unless that truth aligns with the Lord Jesus Christ.

Asking ourselves if we've participated in denial is in itself an indication that perhaps we aren't in denial anymore. A person in denial would immediately slam the door on this statement and say, "That doesn't apply to me." And if you've done that, you might not even be reading this anymore! So if you are still reading, there is good news: you've become willing to explore the possibility. It's like opening the door to a darkened room. Light is going to project itself into the room as much as you are willing to let it. And then those tough questions remain: How much has the addiction controlled me? How have I been living under its terrifying reality?

We fill in the gaps for the addict, making up for what he or she can't do.

Addicts are usually failing to do their God-given duty. And from work to home, addicts often don't need to fulfill their role because someone else is already doing it for them. In fact, an addict needs an overly responsible person in order to function.

Marilyn worked two jobs to support her husband. He had no ambition to find a job and said he was entitled to be at home. He lived off the benefits of his wife's income, while offering very little in return. Marilyn did everything for her husband, and he had no incentive to learn to carry his weight or certainly to stop his addiction. Marilyn unknowingly perpetuated rather than ended the addiction cycle.

Now, there is a catch to this issue. Truth be told, change bears a cost, and it is greater in some situations than in others. Like the addict, you'll need to reach the place where the cost of remaining the same is more painful than the cost of change. In fact, that's where all change begins.

Working through those details may be difficult. If you give up responsibility, you might find yourself homeless and on the street. You can't simply quit a job waiting for ______________ to kick in and support his or her fair share. That makes releasing responsibility extremely difficult for people in marriage. In fact, it requires planning that this material cannot offer.

But let's say you have an adult child living at home. You've offered your child a place to live. You've continued to shower your son or daughter with free amenities. You've even maintained laundry and meals. You may need to prepare to cut some of this off, but not before offering an alternative. Furthermore, if you've overly supported your child, he or she may not have proper life skills. You may need a long-term plan to figure out how to wean your child from your care.

The twelve-step program deals with this area as it encourages an addict to become self-supportive almost immediately. This support may need to be worked out in greater detail as you proceed with an intervention plan.

We excuse the addict's behavior and are willing to blame others for their choices.
When the family supports the addict's behavior, they will look for ways to protect the addict from even having to admit a problem. In fact, this is the most common error parents and close family members make. In their idea of love, they see a good heart underneath the addict and never deal with the wrongful behavior. This protection can become so extreme that if anything or anyone threatens that person, the family can lie and manipulate in the same way as the addict.

Frank was in denial over his wife's problem and didn't want to do anything that would hurt or disrupt her. Thus, when people tried to convince him to get her help, he was defensive. He excused and justified her behavior to the point where he lied and covered for her. In doing so, he was protecting her bondage rather than her freedom. He was serving her addiction every bit as much as she.

TURNING THE CORNER

If you stop enabling, you have essentially removed your finger from the plug, and all the resources to maintain the addiction will drain. You can expect backlash. You should always seek outside assistance if violence or excessive threats could potentially harm you or the addict. It's also important to make adjustments in the tone of love, not shame. In fact, if shame is present, it must first be dealt with before healthy intervention can occur. Your unwillingness to enable the addict isn't a lack of love but a call to use your resources to support a solution. You would rather hurt the addiction and let pain have its perfect work. You are befriending pain only because it will lead your loved one to the hope of change.

Does stopping enabling have a risk? Of course. Addiction can kill, especially addiction to drugs and alcohol. Sadly, not everyone makes it. That's why, when help is wanted, it should always be offered to the struggling addict—as long as it aligns with the addict's sobriety and healing. Not only that, but there is also a time and place to help, and it can be unbelievably hard to know the difference. For example, does the shivering heroin addict that shows up at Mom's house at 2:00 a.m. deserve a warm night's sleep? No one has the answer. It depends strictly on how God moves your heart. The answer isn't what you are going to do in each instance (no one can tell you that; only God knows) but how you manage the relationship over the long haul. You are either promoting a solution—by allowing pain—or demoting a solution by removing it.

Despite how mean it may appear, you know your heart, and you can pray that the addict will eventually understand that what you were doing was, in fact, loving. You are standing up for the real person your loved one is. You are saying, "No way. I'm not a friend of this addiction." This kind of love lets the addict know you are committed to his or her well-being and will not condone the lifestyle of addiction.

Please note: Some people's addictions are more severe than others. Some may involve mental health problems and require immediate professional help. Cutting off a person entirely is not recommended without first seeking guidance, but the goal should be that the addict is not dependent upon you to manage his or her life.

-6-
Waiting for Change

Most of us are tired of waiting, so being asked to wait even more seems disheartening. Who likes a waiting room? Each one of us wants our turn to be released from this difficulty. We may have seen others overcome addiction, but the longer we must wait, the more our situation feels hopeless, unchangeable, and nonnegotiable.

Waiting, therefore, requires a vital ingredient to sustain it: hope. That's why your quiet time with the Lord is so vital: he authors hope and can plant it inside of you. His hope is supernatural; it isn't of this world, and it's not dependent on circumstances. It is formulated from the security he provides despite what happens.

Still, waiting is a discipline like none other. It will squeeze us through a narrow channel filled with darkness, fear, and exhaustion. The Bible talks a great deal about the merit of waiting, and there is a reason for that. Waiting is a dreaded but very real part of our life. That's why we need God's perspective and his help.

> But they who wait for the Lord shall renew their strength; they shall mount up with wings like eagles; they shall run and not be weary; they shall walk and not faint. (Isaiah 40:31 ESV)

> So let's not get tired of doing what is good. At just the right time we will reap a harvest of blessing if we don't give up. (Galatians 6:9)

In the waiting room, there is an active focus we gain, and there is a level of participation that goes above and beyond our effort. This participation involves the fruitful lifestyle of prayer and intercession. Prayer is a resource we've been given to activate God's power on behalf of someone else. If you struggle with

God or don't know how to access him, now is the time to find out why. Look into resources that can help you (we have some resources listed at the end of this article). Invite God to help you explore your own heart and what might be holding you back from trusting him or experiencing him in fullness.

WHEN DESPAIR CLOUDS HOPE

If you find yourself without hope, you are a carrier of deep, deep pain and disappointment. That pain is something God cares about and wants to address. Pain can drive us to seek help. It can also drive us to despair if we don't know what to do with our emotions.

The biblical definition of *despair* is "without resource." This is a place where a person feels so worn out, so used, so taken for granted, and so empty from effort the person feels he or she is without help.

Alongside despair, cynicism can quickly root in our hearts. When we've been hurt over and over again; when days and nights, nights and days seemingly carry on without a response from God; when our circumstances don't change; when we feel we have given everything we have, we can be without resource internally. This pattern can create disbelief in God.

While it's justifiable to feel despair, it is a tragic place for a child of God. You are the recipient of God's love, the object of his affection, even if it doesn't feel that way. Lift your eyes up to heaven right now. Look at the sky and the world around you. Your God created it. He isn't without resource. He has resources—all resources. It may feel as if he's not helping you, but, if so, there is something that needs to be done in your heart.

THE PERIL OF RESENTMENT

People who swim in despair tend to grow bitter, resentful, and angry. Once the heart becomes hardened by resentment, it can be difficult to speak into it. People grow angry because they feel they are powerless victims.

To be a victim of someone else's bad choices is one of the most unjust positions in the world. The reality of the addict's decisions can affect us so much; our lives can spiral downward as if we too are using drugs or alcohol. But to allow our hearts to become contaminated with bitterness is self-destructive.

Breaking away from resentment isn't just a matter of asking for forgiveness. Resentment runs deep. It has pain—deep pain—underneath it. If this applies to you, the hurt that you've experienced and the loss that shadows your hope need to be processed, felt, and validated. Remember, being powerless is being positioned for God's resources. No matter the darkness of our situations, we can make a choice. The choice we have isn't to change the addict or our circumstances but to open our heart to let God replenish the lack in us. It's to give our hurt to him.

No one can tell you to just feel better. No one can tell you, "It's going to be okay." That is a journey you have to choose to engage in. You may fight an internal war that takes you into a pit so intense you don't think light is possible. But look up— you have a Creator and a Redeemer. He is in the pit with you. And he has a way out!

FINDING PEACE

How you gain peace in your life is a choice even if it doesn't feel like one. You don't have to ride the roller coaster with your addict. You can find strength and hope apart from what __________ is doing. At the end of each day, go to that place of quietness we spoke about earlier. You can gain spiritual strength. If you feel too tired, too exhausted, just come as you are. Bring nothing but yourself and the needs you carry. Expect God to give answers. Expect God to come through for you. Listen to worship music, read the Word, and declare out loud what he says. If you are too weak to do that, bring someone with you who can until you gain enough strength—a counselor, a friend, ministry leader, or someone else you trust.

Waiting bears fruit. It will push you into a lifestyle built on faith rather than sight, but not without agony. God is using the pain of your trial to shape you, just as he wants to do for the addict. You might not see the benefits of your pain at first, but God is developing inner strength. He knows that this trial in your life is preparing you for your future. Here's God's promise to you right now. Declare this out loud, and then paste it somewhere to read over and over again:

> There is wonderful joy ahead, even though you have to endure many trials for a little while. These trials will show that your faith is genuine. It is being tested as fire tests and purifies gold—though your faith is far more precious than mere gold. So when your faith remains strong through many trials, it will bring you much praise and glory and honor on the day when Jesus Christ is revealed to the whole world. (1 Peter 1:6–7)

Action Step:
If you feel worn out, tired, and without hope, build your sanctuary. Find a prayer journal to write out anything and everything you feel and experience. Let it out; speak it out. There is no need to hide or place flowery words on your feelings. Coming before God as you are is better than hiding.

Here are some songs to add to your quiet-time collection:

1. "Worn" by Tenth Avenue North

2. "Thy Will" by Hillary Scott

3. "Tell Your Heart to Beat Again" by Danny Gokey

-7-
Building Healthy Boundaries

You have been hurt and violated by the addict in your life. But if you've been trying to help while your loved one has used you, specific actions steps will need to be addressed. Being hurt and feeling pain with God has a sacred place in our healing. However, moving beyond the mode of victimization into empowerment is where strength is found.

God has given you legal rights to be who you are and to be safe from threat and abuse. Did you know that? Indeed, we are sometimes called to suffer, and we are also asked to be sacrificial. But in no way does that mean we can't tend to our personal rights as his children.

Ancient cities of Israel were protected by walls. The people still needed to trust God to protect them; however, they were able to take this action to protect their land and people. The only time they lost protection was when they strayed from God.

In the same way, we can establish personal boundaries around our lives that determine what we let in and what we keep out. A true boundary isn't a means of separation but rather a tool of healthy defense.

While a boundary can appear to be influencing how people treat us, in fact it does no such thing. Healthy boundaries refuse to allow unhealthy people and behaviors from entering our lives. You may say, "It's too late. I have them, and they are here." However, even if they are present in your home, you can take actions to secure and protect yourself in the future. Not only that, but you can also place a shield of God's protection around you even in the midst of the chaos.

If the subject of boundaries seems overwhelming, understand it is not an intellectual concept to grasp. We need to not only learn about boundaries but also have them planted into us in a real and tangible way. It may take additional resources and materials to assist with this process. However, what we can gain right away is some practical application.

DEFINING RIGHTS

The rights you have with the people in your life don't diminish the call to love. Loving people is God's first agenda. But when we are engaged in unhealthy relationships, we will need to maintain a defense system. If we don't understand our fundamental rights, we won't know what we can defend against properly. Let's look at some key areas:

- We have the right to make our choices based on the biblical definition of truth and the guidance of the Holy Spirit. No human being is ever allowed to take that right away from us.
- We have the right to feel our feelings, even if they make other people uncomfortable. Our feelings are not sinful. They are an expression of what is happening within. They may need to heal, but they are not wrong.
- We have the right to say no to lies and manipulation. We do not need to comply with people just because they need something from us. If you find yourself struggling with this, there is deeper work that can be accomplished through a recovery program.
- We have the right to be our true selves—and not to have to change to please others.
- We have the right not to allow or condone sinful behaviors in our relationship. This means we will have to fairly implement boundaries, as will be discussed shortly.
- We have the right to pursue our dreams, care for our well-being, and walk out our God-given destiny. No matter where you are in your relationship, God reserves the right for you to live out your God-given potential. No one can steal that from you unless you allow it.

When we access rights, we have to understand that with them comes responsibly to uphold the rights of others. Here are some areas that contain restrictions:

- We don't have the right to hurt people physically, emotionally, or through any means of abuse.
- We don't have the right to remove other people's mistakes and failures by doing things for them.
- We don't have the right to control people so that they think or do what we want them to.

- We don't have the right to "mind read" and decide for people what they think or feel.
- We don't have the right to make accusations without facts.
- We don't have the right to use guilt, shame, or any form of control to cause people to change.

YOURS AND MINE

A boundary separates two properties. It creates the authorization factor required to be in someone's private space legally. In the addiction cycle, not only can we have our boundaries denied but we can, in turn, also deny the boundary of the addict's individual rights. That's because just as we can define our personal space, we will need to learn to allow ______________ to have the right to his or her space.

More often than not, family members of addicts leave their own property and jump the fence to aid the addict. Unknowingly, they barge through the front door unannounced and begin to clean and perform tasks that have been neglected. These have wide-ranging scenarios as we will begin to discuss in the last chapter. The problem is that as we scrub the addicts' floors, we remove their ability to feel the consequences of their neglect. They don't need to clean their floors if someone else does it on their behalf.

But there's even more. While we are managing their property, we are neglecting our own. In Song of Solomon, a young woman faces this tribulation. She says, "My mother's sons were angry with me and made me take care of the vineyards; my own vineyard I had to neglect" (Song of Solomon 1:6 NIV). That is a picture of enslavement. Put your loved one's name in there, and ask if it applies: "______________ was angry with me and made me take care of his/her life. My own life I had to neglect." If that fits, you are being oppressed.

Whether you are experiencing oppression or simply lack an understanding of boundaries, this crisis becomes twofold. You enable the addiction and neglect your own life. Some of your boundary work is repositioning yourself back to your property and your personal responsibilities. That's difficult! You will need to begin to consciously see what you do that isn't invited or simply never was your job.

If you don't know where to begin, it's helpful to create a three-column page where you can write your name, your family member's name, and God's name. Then define the responsibilities each of you currently has. You can start to go through every facet of your daily life and see how entangled it has become. Ask God for wisdom.

FENCE INTRUSIONS

In active addiction, there are varying levels of violations regarding boundaries. First of all, addicts are very manipulative and cunning in getting what they want and need. They will push their way into our lives to gain access to anything that will help feed their addiction. We've already discussed some of the boundary solutions that apply: we simply stop helping them by cutting off ways that encourage them to keep using.

But our boundary issues will go deeper. We may have an entire system established that has allowed ____________ to intrude on our personal space and our individual rights. The moment we feel unable to make choices because someone is making them on our behalf, we have to step back and assess what's happening.

The reasons we do this vary. Sometimes we have our identity and sense of security so immersed in this person that we assume that if we can fix our loved one, we can also fix ourselves. This is called codependency. It is a mindset that is usually learned early in life. When codependency drives our boundaries, we will be more prone to appease people. Sometimes we'll even change our own beliefs and morals to align with what we think a person wants in a given moment. These moving fences in our lives leave us vulnerable to attacks and crush our sense of value and identity.

Whenever we are unable to say no or feel we have lost our right to make choices for ourselves, we know we need to work through deeper challenges. This isn't an indication that we are flawed, but it usually means we've been hurt. Facing this is difficult, but it will enable us, with the resources, to find hope and healing. There is always a reason for why we do what we do.

Even though you may want to genuinely set boundaries, you might find you are too weak to follow through. That's when you know you need a group or counselor to help you. Your boundaries will need to be affirmed inside you before they can be implemented in your relationships.

DEFINING AND IMPLEMENTING BOUNDARIES

The development of boundaries is simply determining what you will allow and not allow in your life. Writing this out is fairly simple, but you will be challenged by people who will push your boundaries. Thus, setting a boundary is deciding not just what you will allow but what consequence you will impose if someone violates a boundary.

Sometimes the boundary is for you. If you know your areas of weakness, you need to remove yourself from or avoid potentially harmful places, people, and things. Addicts in recovery have to do the same thing: they create boundaries for themselves. They will have to avoid all the places where they could potentially stumble.

But life happens, and people will test boundaries. Boundaries aren't a means to control the behavior of someone else; instead, they have the purpose of personal protection. If you say no and someone doesn't oblige, your boundary will be effective only if you have a means of administering a consequence. Our typical reaction may be anger. In fact, anger by definition is the need to self-preserve because we feel that someone is trying to take or misuse something that belongs to us. Anger also stems from our basic sense of our identity being abused. Anger is justified but is fruitless in and of itself. It is false power that does nothing to change the circumstances.

In addiction, remember that you are loving the addict by allowing him or her to feel the pain of bad choices. Thus, administering consequences is part of that valuable tool. It's also far more effective than simply lashing out in anger.

Consequences empower the boundary and make it valid. If you have no intention of following through on a consequence, your boundary isn't a boundary. It's a false threat. You could later say, "I love _________ so much; I can overlook what he/she did," but you are just allowing the behavior. You have wrongfully defined love. Love isn't a feeling; it's a choice to make the right decision for a person's well-being, not necessarily to appease the person at the moment.

Consequences should be something you can live with. It's common to make empty threats to an addict. It's hard to enforce consequences. But it's vital. A consequence also has to offer itself in proportion to violation. That's why you want to plan your boundaries out in advance and then have a method to enforce them. This works best when you state a clearly defined boundary up front, along with specific consequences to the addict.

If you are married to an addict and are considering major decisions such as separation or divorce, it is strongly advised you seek professional or spiritual counseling or support to work through that decision. It is understandable that you reach a point where you have had enough. Your consequence and breaking points in a relationship, however, should in some way align with God's heart. This is very difficult to navigate. There is forgiveness that needs to be processed even as you are setting boundaries.

Sometimes the right thing to do is to stay and to wait for God to intervene. Other times, you may need to leave temporarily or even permanently if serious situations have occurred. Remember, trampled fences no longer protect. Your boundaries are only as good as your willingness to enforce them.

However, it's vital to understand and remember that, again, boundaries can't control behavior—they simply offer guidelines. We can't tell ____________________ what to do. We can set boundaries in our own property that asks that they respect certain guidelines: Don't come home drunk; don't take _______ without my permission. The boundaries you are entitled to create, however, lie within your space, not someone else's.

Action Step:
Can you think of some boundaries you want stated? About what do you feel most disrespected? That is where you should start.

____
____
____
____
____

BOUNDARIES ARE BRIDGES, NOT WALLS

While boundaries separate our personal rights, they are not intended to act as walls. Simply saying "Do this" and "Don't do that" does very little to promote a healthy relationship. Boundaries are an invitation to learn how to respect, honor, and love each other. They allow us to see and respond to each other's needs and interests.

Enforcing a consequence isn't intended to punish but to offer the opportunity for redemption. People can change. The pain of a consequence is intended to lead to repentance—a change initiated by them, not by our demands.

When people genuinely seek help, actually want change, and are truly sorry, we can administer grace. Grace gives a second chance. It says, "Let's try again." Perhaps you feel you have given grace and grace again. However, there is a dramatic difference between offering authentic grace and simply not having boundaries in the first place. We offer grace when there is true contrition from a lesson learned. The person who violated the boundary is sorry and wants another chance.

If a person is not sorry, then tough decisions need to be made. You cannot have a true relationship with someone who is not sorry for his or her sins. Sin not only separates us from God; it separates us from each other.

It will be a challenge to deal with someone's wrongful behavior without allowing it to contaminate your own heart. We can grow so resentful and angry that we are never able to build a bridge. The work of recovery and healing aids us through this. How you choose to manage the pain of someone's refusal to change his or her destructive habits will define your future. If you choose to remain in bitterness, you have forfeited your ability to find a life despite your loved one's bad choices. But if you choose to work through the addict's violations, you can forge a pathway of redemption for yourself with God's help. The addict has a choice, and you have a choice whether or not to let their bad choices shape your future.

-8-
Developing an Intervention Plan

It's the question you've needed to answer: are you ready? Do you want to put your foot down on someone's addiction? Have you reached your breaking point?

You need to be honest with yourself. Perhaps you can maintain your current circumstance without any intervention. If so, it's strongly advised you enter into a support group. But when you make that decision, consider the children living in the home and how they too have been affected. If you don't know how severe your situation is, consult someone who understands addiction. Sometimes church leaders can give wrongful advice about addiction, encouraging you to put up with anything, no matter what. All this does is encourage a repeat of the cycle over and over again. If you've received that advice, you may want to share this material.

Intervention might not be right for other reasons. There are times you should bypass intervention and seek help immediately. If someone is suicidal or homicidal or exhibits dangerous mental health symptoms, no intervention is necessary; you can admit the addict to the emergency room. However, that person will ultimately have to choose his or her future either way.

For some of you, intervention could be so costly that you have to secure your own life first. That's okay. Be sure to take care of yourself and to be safe before considering intervention. But if you are ready, then intervention is a great tool to help you come against addiction in a loving, truth-based manner. The intervention plan also can be written before a relapse occurs to serve as a form of prevention and planning.

If the addict has never sought help for addiction, you will need to form an intervention plan with a recovery leader, pastor, counselor, or someone else who truly understands addiction. It is essential to learn from others and not take matters into your own hands. If you don't know someone, please call the New Life Spirit Recovery hotline at 866-543-3361. We will help you or find someone who can.

Interventions are typically not successful if only the key family member who has been helping the addict is involved. The addict might not consider the intervention valid. That's not to say it can't happen, however; you'll have to pray and decide what works best.

An intervention tends to be most effective with a team approach. The goal of an intervention is to confront the addict lovingly and graciously. With a team approach, each person involved with the addict expresses his or her love and desire for the addict to get help. But an intervention also includes an explanation of how the addiction has brought each person personal harm and injury. If done with kindness and strength, this is extremely successful. Sometimes the addict can see for the first time how he or she has hurt others.

When you prepare for intervention, you need to be prepared to face a variety of outcomes, including the following:

What will I do if the addict is ready for help?

What does help look like? Are you going to use a program? A twelve-step group? An outpatient option? You need to have your information researched ahead of time and decide the best approach. A residential setting is strongly recommended, but there are other alternatives. You need to do what you are comfortable with if your loved one actually makes the step to seek help.

What will I do if the addict doesn't want help and rejects my offer?

If the addict simply isn't ready to change, you can't change this reality. All you can do is protect your heart and life and enforce the boundaries you set. You'll need to lay down guidelines and consequences for how you are going engage in the relationship. You may need to put the relationship on hold until that person wants or is willing to seek help.

What will I do if the addict wants help but seemingly has little interest in my needs?

Sometimes the intervention can seemingly blow up in your face. Your loved one may get help but also may seem almost spiteful toward you. He or she shuts you out and locks you down. This is frustrating. There are many reasons for that reaction, and getting into a connected group with others dealing with addicts, such as Al-Anon or Celebrate Recovery, is vital. This is a journey that has many twists and turns, and you need to hear from and speak with others on the same pathway. One thing is certain: you'll have the opportunity to enter into your own recovery process so that you can empower yourself to overcome and to be healthy no matter what the addict in your life chooses to do.

PREPARING FOR AN INTERVENTION

If you do a formal intervention (for a person using drugs or alcohol), as soon as the person you love says yes to getting help, you want to have bags packed and be ready to leave immediately (if you choose a residential option). Don't allow any time to lapse unless necessary. There is a strong chance the addict will do whatever is possible to leave to get one more fix. You don't want your loved one out of your sight. If the addict goes into another room, he or she may have drugs already accessible. There can be a more serious tendency to overdose in these circumstances if the addict wants to binge drink or inject a bunch of drugs at one time.

If you are able, coordinate with jobs and have any daycare needs prearranged; this preparation makes the transition easier. Some people may get angry or insulted if you contact an employer, so please use wisdom. If this is a life-threatening addiction, it shouldn't matter. Remember to check local employment laws that protect people with addiction. You can often obtain medical leave without having to reveal details. A treatment facility would help you fill out appropriate paperwork to satisfy those requirements.

On the day of the intervention, you should approach the addict in a prearranged place where everyone is in attendance. At first, the addict will feel tricked and may be bothered. Remember, you are disrupting his or her love affair with ________. That's why you are going to express your love for the person first. Everyone should set the atmosphere with love and support as opposed to anger and shame. Affirmations are very beneficial. The addict will understand that you speak to him or her from a place of value rather than shame.

Assure the addict that everyone will support the healing process and that arrangements can be made to cover needs while he or she is gone. This type of approach stands a very credible chance of working. However, you are still encouraged to use professional guidance when possible.

INTERVENTION CHECKLIST

Please share this with your recovery leader or pastor, and ask for any additional input he or she may have. This is not an all-or-nothing list but rather just helpful ways to begin.

Things to preplan

- Who can I use for a resource to help with an intervention?
- Who should be included in the intervention? Include people who strongly support the addict's well-being and will be able to maintain healthy boundaries.
- Who should not be included in the intervention? Include those people who are extremely bitter or judgmental or would in any way continue to enable your loved one's addiction. People who participate in the intervention cannot take sides.
- What do I need to prepare in advance? (Treatment program, housing, transportation, daycare, employment, medical, finances, etc.)
- What is the plan if the addict agrees? This plan should be a minute-by-minute, hour-by-hour team approach to get the person into a safe setting.
- What is my plan for my safety and security if the intervention doesn't work?

Evaluating my heart

- Preparing for intervention will require your own heart to be properly situated. Ask yourself the following:
- Am I truly surrendered and ready to leave outcomes to God?
- Am I motivated to see ___________ get well, or is this an anger-ridden reaction to try to change the circumstances?
- Am I willing to disrupt what has been normal in our lives? Am I willing to ride out a period of discomfort?
- Will anger or resentment show through in my intervention effort?
- Do I feel ready to embrace pain as a friend rather than a foe?
- Do I need to spend some time getting self-care and finding support before I approach this intervention? How long can it wait, and how urgent a need is it?
- Can I live with this person if nothing changes? What can't I live with?

Sharing with my Addict

Expression is a huge step in a relationship with an addict. So often, feelings are bypassed. The addict can't or won't deal with them. In an intervention, however, feelings need to surface. The more real you can be about your feelings, hurts, and needs, the better.

It's also critical you have the opportunity to express your love for the addict. You may not realize it, but your loved one needs to hear that. In some ways, interacting with the addict is like wrestling with an impostor version of who he or she is. Buried underneath the addict is the person you love—and all the God-given potential he or she has as a spouse, friend, parent, child, sibling, etc.

To help you prepare to share your heart with the addict in the intervention, on a separate piece of paper, write out the following answers as if you are talking to ______________:

- I want you to know this is how I see you and love you. This is your potential, and this is the future I see for you without [name the drug or behavior] ______________.
- I want you to know this is how you have hurt me. (Be very specific and heartfelt.)
- This is what I will no longer allow in my life due to your addiction.
- This is how I value our relationship.
- This is how difficult it has been for me to watch you self-destruct.
- This is what changes when you are ______________.
- I don't want to watch you hurt yourself or me anymore. You need help. (Use your own words to express this.)
- If you aren't willing to get help, this is where I stand with our relationship.

Writing the Letter

Once you have gathered your thoughts, it is important that you write a personalized letter that includes the points you've discovered are most important. Part of this process prepares your heart because you may not even realize what you will say until you start writing. You will be surprised how much pain comes up when you write this. But something else may occur: you may find yourself very angry and hardened. If this occurs, it's vital that you seek support before you proceed. If an intervention is done out of anger, even though your feelings are understandable, it could have a catastrophic effect. When anger surfaces, keep writing it out. However, don't use that letter for the intervention itself. Your feelings of anger are valid! It's just better to work some of it out before you engage than to spew it out and ruin the chances of a positive intervention process.

If you are considering writing a letter on your own, be sure to first seek advice from someone who understands the addiction cycle. Your letter should exclude any control or direct statement that dictates what the addict should do; rather, it should be an invitation for him or her to seek help and a clear boundary of what you will no longer tolerate.

Presenting the Intervention

The moment of the intervention could be a life-changing event, or it could drive the person back into addiction. That's why you need to make up your mind beforehand about how you will handle future situations. If the person isn't ready, he or she needs more pain. If the person rejects help but is allowed to remain with the same provisions as before, the intervention will have zero power and no effect. And chances are, the addict knows that. Instead, when the day arrives, you have to ask yourself how ready you are for change and how willing you are to disrupt your lifestyle to show the addict you are not going to condone or excuse his or her bad choices.

Margaret's intervention didn't go as planned. Even though the family perfectly followed guidelines and felt they all made a strong case, she simply didn't want to oblige. Her heartbroken husband struggled with the next step. He hadn't been fully prepared for her to say no. Thus, he packed his bags and took the kids with him to his parents' house, where he began the process of legal separation. Margaret was shocked that he took such extreme measures and made his life so inconvenient. She binged for several days, but the empty house was a haunting reminder of her decision, and she eventually did get help.

Jennifer's husband's intervention didn't go as well. When she made steps to request her husband leave the family home, she was tempted to retreat. But the stronger her boundaries, the more her husband fought. His lack of brokenness remained. She needed to move on with her life at some point because not only was he drinking but he was also unfaithful to their wedding vows. Thus, she had to fully engage in a plan for herself and the protection of her children. It involved taking steps to find a job, family support, and a specific way to end her marriage. Do we advocate that for everybody? No! However, if someone is abusive, unfaithful, and unbroken, that may be a direction you'll have to go.

Thankfully, there are good outcomes too! Joshua received the help he needed. He went on to treatment and dealt with his childhood wounding.

He became a new man. When his wife, Susan, saw his change, she had mixed feelings. He was a person she no longer recognized.

You may be surprised that if your intervention is successful and the person in your life finds freedom, you will still struggle. It will almost feel as if the pain you've experienced is invalidated: the addict moves on, happy and free, while you are still trying to pick up broken pieces.

The best thing you can do for yourself is to be honest about what you need right now. If you find hope and healing, you'll be able to help ____________ walk the pathway of healing too. But if you hold on to your pain and anger, you may fight against your loved one's well-being. While this outcome may seem strange, it's actually more common than not. The majority of divorces happen when the addict gets sober. The best way to prevent this result is for both family and addict to acquire support systems in recovery.

WHERE TO GO NEXT

While you've focused on the intervention needs of the person with the addiction, God has focused on intervening with you. As absurd as it may sound, the very difficulty of your situation can be a doorway to a deeper and more fulfilling life. The level of hurt you experience is the level of grace and healing that God can pour into you.

This is a season for you to develop self-confidence and a strategy to live above the addiction's grip on you personally. There are resources to help you. If you are in a strained marriage, you'll have to make very difficult decisions. It's going to require establishing painful boundaries. But you can do it! You don't have to be a victim of someone else's poor choices. God can empower you!

DO YOU FEEL ALONE?

You may feel you've been thrown onto an island. You may feel isolated in the shame and lack of acceptance of addiction by your friends and family. That's why you need to know something: addiction is unbelievably common. There is a 100 percent chance that others you know are going through the same thing but are too afraid to admit it. Addiction is so common that everyone you meet will most likely know at least one addict.

Did you know that:

- Over fifteen million people abuse or are dependent on alcohol?
- Over twenty million people are abusing illicit drugs?
- Over forty million people are involved in Internet sex, and over ten

million have an addiction?

Yes, addiction is far from unusual, and you are far from alone. But you feel alone. That's why your number one goal is to be connected with those who know what you feel and won't judge you.

ASK FOR HELP

There are countless family support groups through twelve-step anonymous programs such as Al-Anon. Celebrate Recovery is also expanding across the country and the world, offering you a Christian perspective. Search local listings for these programs.

New Life Spirit Recovery has an outreach ministry that offers resources to those who need coaching through this process. We have chaplains and counselors who have worked with countless others to navigate this process.

If you need to talk to an admission adviser regarding a treatment program for someone you love, please call us directly at 866-543-3361. We have a team of professionals who can assist you immediately and help you develop a plan. If we can't help you, we'll find someone who can.

ADDITIONAL RESOURCES THROUGH SPIRIT OF LIFE AND NEW LIFE SPIRIT RECOVERY

New Life Spirit Recovery Treatment Program
We offer professional, affordable treatment programs for addiction. We have thirty-day, sixty-day, and ninety-day programs. Go to www.newlifespiritrecovery.com for more information.

Breaking Point Intervention Coaching
We will assess your situation and help you develop a specific plan, including boundaries and all the steps discussed in this article. Go to www.spiritofliferecovery.com and click on Interventions.

Intervention Workshops and Classes
Intervention workshops are held on a regular basis. If we don't have a current group, you can still sign up for a past workshop to receive the material and videos.

Books
Christian Families in Recovery: A Guide to Intervention through God's Tools of Intervention
This is our complete workbook on the addiction and treatment process. Available on Amazon.

The Christian Codependence Workbook and Workshops: From Surviving to Significance
This is a very popular book used throughout the recovery and church community. It specifically addresses the nature and removal of codependence. Available on Amazon.

A House That Grace Built: Moving Beyond Codependence to Embrace God's Design for Love, Intimacy, and Wholeness

This book details the intensive process of learning how to establish healthy boundaries in our relationship to others. It highlights areas such as intimacy, forgiveness, redemption, boundaries, and securing our future. Available on Amazon.

Codependence Recovery Workshops
We host education and healing workshops based on the previous listing. We

also have recordings of past workshops available so you can be self-paced. Go to www.spiritofliferecovery.com to find out more.

Healing Workshops

We offer online workshops that deal with healing the hurt of the past. These workshops aren't specific to an issue; they address the pain of the past. Please look for Healing Intensives in the near future. Visit www.spiritofliferecovery.com to learn more.

Outpatient Counseling for Non-Substance Needs

We offer one-on-one outpatient and online counseling for family members of someone struggling with addiction. Counseling is also available for any matter of the heart. We do not use these services for someone in active addiction because that requires more oversight than our outpatient services can offer through our ministry, including drug testing. All active addiction should be referred to New Life Spirit Recovery. To learn more about counseling, visit www.spiritofliferecovery.com and click on Counseling.

This entire book was modified based on the material from Christian Families in Recovery. We encourage you to purchase the entire workbook for a comprehensive approach. You can find it through Amazon and other online retailers.

Made in the USA
Middletown, DE
03 September 2020